KARATE

NEIL MORRIS

HEINEMANN LIBRARY
CHICAGO, ILLINOIS

© 2001 Reed Educational & Professional Publishing
Published by Heinemann Library,
an imprint of Reed Educational & Professional Publishing,
Chicago, Illinois

Customer Service 888-454-2279

Visit our website at www.heinemannlibrary.com

Designed by Ken Vail Graphic Design, Cambridge
Illustrations by Simon Girling & Associates (Mike Lacey)
Originated by Dot Gradations
Printed by Wing King Tong in Hong Kong.

05 04 03 02 01
10 9 8 7 6 5 4 3 2 1

Library of Congress Cataloging-in-Publication Data
Morris, Neil, 1946-
  Karate / Neil Morris.
     p. cm. -- (Get going! Martial arts)
Includes bibliographical references (p.) and index.
  ISBN 1-58810-039-1
  1. Karate--Juvenile literature. [1. Karate.] I. Title.
  GV1114.3 .M647 2001
  796.815'3--dc21
                          00-013255

Acknowledgments
The Publishers would like to thank the following for permission to reproduce photographs: Action Plus/R. Francis, p. 5; Blitz, p. 8; Silvio Dokov, p. 29; Robert Harding, p. 7. All other photographs by Trevor Clifford.

Cover photograph reproduced with permission of Sporting Images, Australia.

Every effort has been made to contact copyright holders of any material reproduced in this book. Any omissions will be rectified in subsequent printings if notice is given to the Publisher.

The Publisher would like to thank Head Instructor Greg Scott, of Shotokan Karate of America, for helping us improve the accuracy of this text.

Some words are shown in bold, **like this.** You can find out what they mean by looking in the glossary.

Japanese words are shown in italics, *like this.* You can find out what they mean by looking at the chart on page 30.

CONTENTS

> **!** Please remember that martial arts need to be taught by a qualified, registered teacher. Do not try any of the techniques and movements in this book without such an instructor present.

WHAT IS KARATE?

Karate is a Japanese martial art that developed many years ago as a form of self-defense. The word *karate* means "empty hand," because it uses no weapons. Instead, the hands and feet are used to make powerful punches, strikes, and kicks, as well as to block the opponent's attacks. Today, most attacking moves are pulled, or held back, so that the opponent is not actually hit, because this would be painful and could be dangerous.

Karate is considered a way of life by many who study it. Karate teaches young people to focus their minds, and helps them become more self-confident. It makes them strong in mind and body. At the same time, it teaches techniques of self-defense and is a high-energy form of exercise.

There are many recognized karate clubs with experienced teachers throughout the United States.

WHERE TO LEARN AND PRACTICE

This book tells you how to get started in karate. It also shows and explains some karate techniques, so that you can understand and practice them. But always remember that you cannot learn a martial art just from a book. To study karate seriously, you must go to regular lessons with a qualified teacher, so that you learn all the techniques properly and then repeat and practice them many times.

MAIN KARATE STYLES

- *Shotokan*, which means "Shoto's house," is one of the most popular karate styles. *Shoto* was the **pen name** of the founder of karate. His students trained at his house. Most of the photographs in this book are based on the *Shotokan* style.

- *Gojo ryu*, or "hard/soft school," teaches a program of fitness training to help students improve their strength, endurance, and speed. It was founded by Chojun Miyagi.

- *Wado ryu*, "way of peace school," was founded by Hironori Ohtsuka, one of the strongest students in "Shoto's house." Its fast actions are intended to avoid or withstand the force of an opponent.

- *Kyokushinkai*, "way of ultimate truth," was founded by Masutatsu Oyama.

- *Shotokai*, "Shoto's way," is a later style that returned to more traditional ways, with very little competition and **free sparring** that is not related to competition.

- *Shito ryu* was founded by Kenwa Mabuni, a policeman from Okinawa. He named the style after his two teachers.

YOUR KARATE CLUB

Choose your club carefully. It should have an experienced teacher, and it should belong to a karate association. The list on page 31 shows where you can get more information about karate clubs.

Karate is enjoyed by boys and girls, and men and women, of all ages.

KARATE—THE BEGINNINGS

The martial art of karate began hundreds of years ago on the island of Okinawa, over which China and Japan fought for many centuries. Young men from Okinawa visited China and brought back with them some of the ancient techniques of Chinese boxing. In 1609, the Japanese took over the island and banned the local people from carrying weapons. This led the Okinawans to develop their unarmed fighting style further, especially as a means of self-defense.

GICHIN FUNAKOSHI

Okinawa officially became part of Japan in 1879, when a young Okinawan named Gichin Funakoshi was just eleven years old. Funakoshi studied the martial arts of the island, and by the early 1900s he was giving private, and then public, demonstrations of the art he called karate.

In 1917, Funakoshi was invited to the main islands of Japan to demonstrate karate. He later performed karate for the Japanese emperor. Funakoshi stayed in Japan for the rest of his life, writing books on the martial art under the **pen name** *Shoto.*

This map shows Okinawa, an island near China and the islands of Japan.

These figures show ancient Chinese boxing. Karate was later developed from this form of unarmed fighting.

SHOTOKAN KARATE

Funakoshi finally opened his own karate training center, located in his house, and called it *Shotokan,* or "Shoto's house." This became the name of his style of karate, which is still one of the most popular styles in the world.

After World War II ended in 1945, many American soldiers served in Japan. They brought their knowledge of karate back to the United States and opened karate schools. It was not long before some of the schools formed world organizations. Some organizations made rules to run karate as a sport.

KARATE WORLD CHAMPIONSHIPS

The first world championships were held in Tokyo, Japan, in 1970, and the first individual and team events were won by the Japanese. Ten years later, weight categories were introduced for men, and the first women's event was staged—and won by a Japanese contestant.

Today, competitors take part in different world championships given by many organizations every year. Students all over the world enjoy learning about and practicing the art of karate.

EQUIPMENT

Karate is practiced and performed in a white outfit called a *karategi,* or *gi* (sounds like *gee*) for short. It is best to buy a *gi* through your club, but you do not need to have one right away. For the first few sessions, a sweatshirt and sweatpants or a T-shirt and jogging pants will do.

The *gi* is all white. It is made up of a pair of trousers and a loose jacket tied at the waist with a belt. Girls wear a white T-shirt under the jacket. *Gis* are usually sold with a white belt, which is normally the right color for a beginner. Make sure that your *gi* is large enough so that your movements will not be restricted in any way. The trouser legs should not touch the ground. Keep in mind that they will probably shrink when washed.

It is very important to take good care of your *gi.* Always keep it clean. Wash and iron it regularly, and fold it carefully after each training session. A neat and tidy appearance shows that you have the right attitude toward training. Inside the training hall, called a *dojo,* you must always have bare feet. A pair of flip-flops is useful to keep your feet clean as you walk from the changing room to the *dojo.*

PROTECTIVE EQUIPMENT

Some styles of karate may require protective equipment, depending on their goals and rules. The most important are fist mitts, also called hand pads, and shin and instep pads. It is also a good idea for boys to wear a protective cup. Both boys and girls should wear mouthguards when participating in competitions.

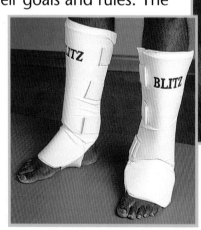

Fist mitts, shin pads, and instep pads help to keep you safe.

PUTTING ON THE GI

1 Put the trousers on first. Many *gi* bottoms have elastic at the waist. If they have a drawstring, pull it, and tie it with a bow. Next, put on the jacket, crossing the left side over the right side.

2 To tie the belt, pull it across your stomach first, keeping the two ends at an equal length.

3 Cross the ends over at the back, and bring them back to the front.

4 Cross the left end over the right, then pull it up behind both layers of the belt.

5 Finally, tie the free ends together right over left and pull them through to finish the knot.

 SAFETY

In order not to harm yourself or anyone else, do not wear a watch or any jewelry. Keep your fingernails and toenails trimmed short. Pull long hair back, but do not use metal clips.

Make sure that you are in good shape for active exercise, and do not train if you are ill. Getting a little tired in a class is part of training, but exercise should not hurt. Never push yourself to a point at which you feel pain.

Any martial art can be dangerous if it is not performed properly. Never fool around inside or outside the training hall—or at home or in school—by showing off or pretending to have a real fight.

IN THE DOJO

It is important for any *karateka,* or karate student, to show respect and courtesy to everyone and everything to do with karate, including the *dojo,* or training hall. Always bow to your instructor or to the **senior grade** *karetakas* when you go into the *dojo.* If there is no one in the *dojo* when you enter, stop inside the entrance and bow to the middle of the hall. Always do the same when you leave the hall.

THE STANDING BOW

You also make the standing bow before and after every exercise, and to your opponent before and after each contest. Put your heels together and place your hands flat against your thighs. Then bow smoothly by bending your upper body forward, but not too far. Count to two as you hold that position. Always look at the person to whom you are bowing. Then straighten up again, move your feet apart, and clench your fists.

Courtesy is a traditional and important part of karate. One way of showing courtesy is the standing bow.

THE KNEELING BOW

At the beginning of a training session, all students perform a kneeling bow to the *sensei,* or teacher. The senior grade will call out "*Seiza!*"—"Kneel!" Place your left knee on the floor, with your hands flat on your thighs. Bring your right knee down, point your toes, and sit back on your calves, keeping your back straight and looking forward. As the senior grade shouts "*Sensei ni rei!*"—"Bow to the teacher!"—the class performs the kneeling bow together.

All karate students perform the kneeling bow before training.

From the kneeling position, put your hands or fists down on the floor in front of you and bend your upper body into a low bow. Count to two and then return to an upright kneeling position. After you bow, the teacher will bow to the class.

When the senior grade calls out "*Otagai ni rei!*"—"Bow to your classmates!"—do another kneeling bow to the other *karatekas.* They will then bow to you. At the call of "*Kiritsu!*" or "*Koritz!*"—"Stand up!"—lift your left knee, then your right knee, and return to standing at attention.

WARMING UP

Karate involves a lot of physical exercise. It is important to warm your body up and stretch your muscles before training so that you do not injure yourself. At your club, you will always start a session with some warm-up exercises. You might begin by walking or jogging in place for a couple of minutes before doing some stretching exercises.

TRICEPS STRETCH

The tricep is the large muscle at the back of the upper arm.

1 Standing up straight, raise your right arm and touch your right shoulder with your fingertips.

2 Push your left hand gently against your right elbow.

3 Lower your fingers down your back as far as you can without hurting yourself, and hold that position for a count of eight.

4 Repeat the stretch with your left arm raised.

ARM CIRCLES

1 Stand up straight with your feet placed a shoulder-width apart.

2 Stretch your arms out to the sides at shoulder level and then rotate them in forward circles. Do ten circles, making them as wide as you can.

3 Repeat the ten circles, this time backwards.

CALF STRETCH

The calf muscle is at the back of your lower leg.

1 Stand up straight and put one foot about 12 inches (30 centimeters) ahead of the other.

2 Raise the toes of your forward foot as far as you can, keeping your heel firmly on the floor. Hold this position for a count of ten.

3 Repeat the stretch with your other leg.

! IMPORTANT

- Drink a lot of water, and do not exercise too hard when it is very hot or humid.

- Never exercise when you are ill or injured.

- Try not to breathe too hard and fast when you are exercising, warming up, or cooling down.

- Do not hold your breath while you are exercising.

- When you are stretching, you should always remain comfortable, and your muscles should not hurt. If you feel pain, stop at once.

- Begin to exercise immediately after warming up. Do some cool-down activities immediately after you exercise.

PUNCHING

In karate, your main weapon is the closed fist, which is used to punch. It is important to make a fist correctly, so that your punch is as powerful as possible but does not hurt you, the striker. Power comes from having the fist, wrist, elbow, shoulder, and other parts of your body all acting together. You can practice this by punching a special pad held up by your opponent. Remember, when you punch in a **sparring session,** your fist must stop just short of your opponent so that he or she is not actually touched. Fist mitts are important in case you do accidentally strike your opponent.

MAKING A FIST

1 To make a fist, first fold your fingers down. Then fold your thumb across the index and middle fingers, to lock them in.

2 In a karate punch, you aim at the target with the first two knuckles. Keep your fist straight, in line with your lower arm, so that the wrist does not bend when you hit the target. But keep your arm slightly bent at the elbow when you punch, so as not to put too much strain on your elbow.

Making a fist must be done properly to avoid injury.

! When making a fist, never put your thumb inside your fingers. If your thumb is on the inside, it can be badly hurt, or even broken, when you punch.

PRACTICING THE BASIC PUNCH

1 Start in the attention **stance,** with your heels together and your palms on your thighs. Move into the ready stance by stepping to the side with the left foot, followed by the right foot. Make closed fists in front of you.

2 Move your feet farther apart and bend your knees so that you are in a horse-riding stance. Push your right fist forward, with the palm downward. Then pull your left fist to your side, turning the palm upward.

3 Pull your right fist back, and at the same time push your left fist forward, so that your two fists pass each other in front of you.

4 Before your right arm reaches your body, turn it so that the palm is upward. At the same time, turn your left fist around into the punching position and make a punching motion with it.

5 Go back to the beginning and repeat the punch up to ten times. Then change over so that you punch with your right fist. Repeat this exercise ten times.

KICKING

In karate, kicks are even more powerful weapons than punches. Kicks have a greater reach, but because they have to travel a long way to hit their target, an opponent has more time to avoid them. Most karate kicks begin with the leg bent at the knee. The leg is then straightened to hit the target with the foot, but never with the toes. It is important to keep the leg slightly bent, so as not to put too much strain on the knee.

These are four of the more basic kicks.

FRONT KICK

1 You will probably learn this kick first. Start off in the ready **stance,** shown on page 15, and then slide your left foot forward. Bend your knees and keep your left fist up to guard your face.

2 Bring your right leg forward and raise your right foot, pulling the toes back.

3 When your right knee is high, thrust out your right leg, pushing your hips into the kick. Imagine you are hitting the target, your opponent's chest, with the ball of your foot—the hard part of your foot just below the toes. Keep your guard up during the kick.

4 After the kick, pull your leg back quickly and put your foot down on the floor in as controlled a way as possible.

SIDE KICK

1 With this kick, you hit the target with your heel and the little toe edge of your foot. Start with your legs apart and your knees bent, and hold your clenched fists at your thighs.

2 Lean to the left, away from the target, and raise your right knee across your body. Point the heel of your right foot directly at the target and then drive your leg out in a straight, thrusting action. As you do this, it is important to lift your big toe and turn down the other toes on the kicking foot.

BACK KICK

1 This kick involves turning your back on your opponent, so you should only use it as a surprise move or after another attacking technique.

2 Keep your eyes on your opponent as you lift your right foot and thrust it back in a straight line, heel first.

ROUNDHOUSE KICK

1 With this kick, you can strike with either the instep or the ball of the foot, curling around into the side of your target. If you are very close to the target, you can use your shin.

2 Point your toes as you bring your left knee up and across your body. Twist on your supporting leg and kick across the front of your body, straightening your ankle as much as possible and keeping your toes turned down.

BLOCKING

In any martial art, players have to learn to defend themselves against attacks by their opponent. Even the best attacking *karatekas* also need good defending technique. All the basic moves in karate start with a block, which is used to defend an attack by the opponent.

There are different types of blocks, including the knife and scooping blocks. Using blocks reminds the *karateka* that the true spirit of karate is not to strike the first blow but to defend against aggression. A good block will upset the opponent's balance and force him or her into a position in which he or she is open to a **counter-attack.**

KNIFE BLOCK

This block protects the face and chest, using the little-finger edge of the hand to deflect, or turn away, a punch or strike. The blocking hand is open and flat, with the fingers pressed together and the thumb pressed into the side of the hand. This "knife hand" is similar to the "karate chop" that a lot of people associate with karate.

1 Take up the ready **stance.** Slide your right foot forward and put your right arm up, with the palm facing forward.

2 Step forward with your left foot, drop your right arm so that your hand faces forward, and bring your left hand to the right side of your face.

3 Draw your right hand back to your chest and face your left palm toward the blow coming from your opponent, keeping your left arm bent.

4 Block the strike with the outside of your left hand and push it away and down to the left, with a cutting action. This is why this move is often called a knife block.

SCOOPING BLOCK

This is a good defense against a front kick.

1 As your opponent lifts his or her foot to kick, twist your hips so that you are turned sideways. Bring your left hand around and under your opponent's ankle to deflect the kick.

2 Your opponent will now be off-balance, and you can take a punch with your right hand.

JAPANESE NUMBERS

In karate, counting is often done in Japanese.

Number:		Sounds like:	Number:		Sounds like:
One	*ichi*	ee-chee	Six	*roku*	rokoo
Two	*ni*	nee	Seven	*shichi*	she-chee
Three	*san*	san	Eight	*hachi*	ha-chee
Four	*shi*	she	Nine	*ku*	kee-oo
Five	*go*	go	Ten	*ju*	joo

COMBINATIONS

Combination techniques link punching, kicking, and blocking moves together in a series. This is when karate becomes more like a real contest. A defender might find it easy to block separate punches or kicks, but it is more difficult to defend against a series of them aimed at different parts of the body and coming from different angles.

At first, you will follow combinations taught by your instructor. He or she will make sure that each individual technique is done correctly before the next one is added. As you become more experienced, you can add a greater number of more difficult techniques. Eventually, you will be able to make up your own combinations, using the techniques that suit you best. Practice them in front of a mirror to see if you are making any mistakes. It is a good idea to choose a different target for each technique, so that the defender has to keep finding different blocks. You must be able to use your combinations when you are advancing and attacking or retreating and defending.

FRONT KICK AND REVERSE PUNCH

This is a simple combination.

1 First front kick with your left leg, as on page 16. Then put your leg down in a forward-facing position.

2 Pull back your left arm and punch strongly with your right fist. This is called a reverse punch because the punching arm is on the same side as the back foot.

KATA

Kata means "pattern," or "form." It is a series of set moves to improve technique and help a *karateka* learn about attack, defense, and **counter-attack.** The moves are like training drills with an imaginary opponent.

At first, each *kata* is practiced in single moves, so that students can learn and memorize each one. Then the moves are built into a sequence, with a pause before each new one. Finally, the students perform the *kata* all the way through, imagining that they are reacting to an attacker or group of attackers. Experienced *karatekas* flow through the complete drill, concentrating their attention, avoiding any hesitation, and remaining balanced throughout the routine.

It will take many hours of practice before you reach this level. Then you will remember the sequences automatically and can concentrate on the imaginary contest.

This karateka *is showing three moves from a* kata.

SPARRING

Combination techniques lead to the next aspect of karate, called *kumite,* which means "sparring." This allows you to test the skills you have learned and practiced on an opponent. At first all the sparring is pre-arranged, which means that both opponents agree beforehand what they are going to do. This makes the contest much safer.

FIVE-STEP SPARRING

Five-step sparring, or *gohon kumite,* is used to practice basic attacks and blocks. Both *karatekas* know which attacks and blocks will be used, so they can each concentrate fully on their moves. After the fifth step, the two *karatekas* bow to each other and change roles.

These karatekas *are practicing their moves during five-step sparring.*

KIAI

The *kiai* is a short, loud shout made at the end of any powerful karate move. It sounds like "Eee!" or "Hai!," and it shows that your mind and body are working together in harmony. The *kiai* helps to give power to your move, gives you confidence, and scares your opponent.

! SPARRING SAFETY

When you are sparring with another *karateka,* you must concentrate very hard and make sure that you do not actually hit your opponent. The balance you learned during all those hours of practice will help you maintain proper control. Always work with your opponent, so that you help each other practice and learn together. Remember that you are responsible for your own safety as well as your opponent's.

SEMI-FREE SPARRING

In this next stage of karate, both students know what sort of attack is going to be made, but the defender is allowed to choose his or her blocks and responses. For example, the attacker may be allowed to use only one kind of kick, such as the roundhouse kick. He or she can, however, change legs and aim at different parts of the opponent's body. The defender can use any blocking technique he or she wishes.

Semi-free sparring is a good way to practice both attacking and defending moves.

! COOLING DOWN

It is important to cool down gently after high-energy exercise such as karate. You can do this by jogging or walking, breathing deeply, and doing gentle stretching exercises like those you used to warm up on pages 12–13. Some *karatekas* also like to cool down by doing some slow *kata* exercises.

GRADING

When you join some karate clubs, you are given a license book as part of your membership. You use the license book to record your progress through each karate grade, called *kyu*. In other clubs you will be given a certificate after each exam. Each grade has a different color belt. You will probably start at the ninth *kyu* and you can then work your way up to first *kyu*.

This student is being given a license book by an instructor at her club.

BELT RANKS

Grades and belt colors vary between karate schools. The following is a system used by some schools.

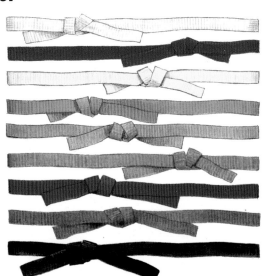
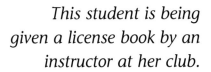

Belt color	Kyu (grade)
white	10th or ungraded
red	9th
yellow	8th
orange	7th
green	6th
blue	5th
purple	4th
brown	3rd, 2nd, and 1st
black	highest grade

At each grade, there is a different set of karate techniques to learn. To move up to the next grade, you have to show that you have learned these completely. This is tested in a grading exam, which may be given by your instructor. You will have to perform basic karate techniques and certain *katas.* You will also do some sparring. Exams may take place from every month or two to once or twice a year, depending on the school.

Grading exams determine whether students are ready to move up to the next grade.

BROWN AND BLACK BELTS

A brown belt is a **senior grade.** It is made up of three *kyu* levels, third to first, through which every *karateka* must progress before aiming for the black belt. The black belt is the highest color you can earn, but it is just the beginning of serious training. Schools split the black belt up into different *dans,* or degrees. Some schools divide it into five *dans,* but some have up to ten. The *karateka* must train for years between each *dan.* Even after earning the highest *dan,* the *karateka* continues to study and improve.

It usually takes four or five years for a *karateka* to earn a black belt. This varies according to the rules of the karate club, however, and may depend on how often the *karateka* trains. Grades are important and are to be respected, but you will notice that expert *karatekas* show complete respect for lower grades and beginners too. This is an important aspect of all the martial arts. You should not worry too much about your belt color. Do your best, and you will advance at your own pace, whatever age you are when you begin.

COMPETITION

There are many different views about competition in karate. Some people believe that sparring is the ultimate aim of all *karatekas.* Others think personal development is more important. This book presents basic information about the sport of karate on the pages that follow, but there are other forms of competition as well.

KATA COMPETITIONS

Your karate club or regional association may hold *kata* competitions. These are organized into age and grade categories. The *katas* are watched by a panel of judges, who give scores on a scale from one to ten. In some *kata* competitions, there are three rounds.

FREE SPARRING

Karatekas are not allowed to try **free sparring**—in which the moves are not known beforehand—until they can perform all the basic techniques well and with confidence. Nothing is gained by sparring before you are ready, and it could be dangerous. In addition, not all karate students like free sparring. Many prefer to stick to set routines.

Karatekas *wait until they are comfortable with basic karate techniques before they try free sparring.*

Sparring partners should be the same grade. You may wear protective equipment for sparring, depending on your school's goals and rules. You are not allowed to attack your opponent's shin, ankle, knee, or groin, and you must be careful not to hurt an opponent. If you ever feel that your opponent is losing control and trying to hurt you, step back, bow, and go sit cross-legged at the side of the *dojo*.

KUMITE COMPETITIONS

Some karate clubs concentrate on sparring, and spend a lot of time training for *kumite* competitions. These are held in age and grade categories, and sometimes in height or weight categories. Boys and girls compete separately.

In these competitions, points are awarded by judges for speed, accuracy, and correct technique. A match is usually two minutes long, and the first person to score three points wins. Otherwise, at the end of the match, the *karateka* with the most points wins. There is an **arbitrator** and a set of referees for each match. To score a point, you must strike within 2 inches (5 centimeters) of the target area—head, chest, and stomach—without the punch or kick being blocked. Referees can also award half-points.

A karateka must hit the target areas, shown in gray, to score.

A WORLD SPORT

Karate can also be part of international sport competition. Some organizations have world championships with many classes and categories. There are team and individual competitions for men and women. Usually contestants are divided into weight categories.

CONTESTS

Karate contests take place on an 8¾-yard- (8-meter-) square mat or floor space. Each match is controlled by a referee and a judge. They stand on the mat and move around it so that they always have a good view of the match. The length of matches can vary, but most last from two to three minutes. The referee makes all final decisions, but he or she may ask the judge's opinion if necessary. An extra **arbitrator** sits outside the contest area. He or she may be asked to help make a decision. A timekeeper and a scorer also sit outside the match area.

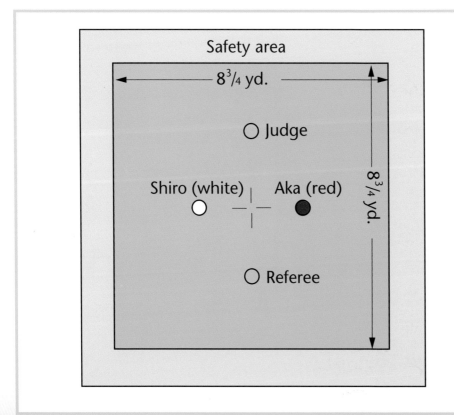

This diagram shows the layout of a typical karate match area.

THE POINTS SYSTEM

One of the two contestants wears a white belt and is referred to as *shiro*, Japanese for "white." The other competitor wears a red belt and is called *aka,* or "red." To win, a contestant has to score a certain number of points that is determined before the match. If neither does so in the time allowed, the one who has more points than his or her opponent wins. All points are scored by strikes to the opponent's target area. This includes the head and the upper body, but not the arms or the tips of the shoulders. No contact to the throat or groin is allowed, and no physical contact is required for scoring. Light contact is allowed on the body. Only very light contact is allowed on the head.

The two contestants exchange blows, blocks, attacks, and **counter-attacks** until one of them achieves a strike. A full point, or *ippon,* is awarded for a blow that is struck with good form, correct attitude, high energy, alertness of mind, proper timing, and from the correct distance. A half point, or *waza-ari,* is awarded for a blow that is effective but not executed quite as well. Penalties are awarded for fouls and breaking the rules, which usually result in half a point or a point being given to the opponent. Too much physical contact will result in the contestant being disqualified.

Karate is a very popular sport, involving major world and national competitions.

JAPANESE WORDS

The Japanese words are pronounced as written here. When you see the letters *ai*, say them like the English word *eye*.

Japanese word	Meaning	Japanese word	Meaning
aka, or *akai*	red	*Kyokushinkai*	way of ultimate truth
dan	degree		
dojo	training hall	*kyu*	grade
gohon kumite	five-step sparring	*otagai ni rei*	bow to your classmates
Gojo ryu	hard/soft school	*seiza*	kneel
		sensei	teacher
ippon	full point	*sensei ni rei*	bow to the teacher
karategi	karate outfit		
karateka	karate student	*shiro*	white
kata	pattern, form	*Shito ryu*	Shito school
kiai	explosive shout that gives power	*Shotokai*	Shoto's way
		Shotokan	Shoto's house
		Wado ryu	way of peace school
koritz	stand up		
kumite	sparring	*waza-ari*	half point

GLOSSARY

arbitrator	senior referee who judges a karate contest
counter-attack	attack that replies to an attack by an opponent
free sparring	practice contest between two karate students in which the moves are not known beforehand
pen name	name a person uses that is not his or her real name
senior grade	experienced karate student who is at a high level or grade
sparring session	period of time in which two karate students have a practice contest, sometimes with the moves agreed upon beforehand
stance	position of the body, with the feet in a particular place and the arms held in a particular way

MORE BOOKS TO READ

Jensen, Julie. *Beginning Karate*. Minneapolis, Minn.: Lerner Publishing Group, 1998.

Randall, Pamela. *Karate*. New York: Rosen Publishing Group, Inc., 1999.

Schwartz, Stuart, and Craig Conley. *Karate Blocks*. Mankato, Minn.: Capstone Press, 1998.

Schwartz, Stuart, and Craig Conley. *Karate Kicks*. Mankato, Minn.: Capstone Press, 1998.

TAKING IT FURTHER

Martial Arts Masters World Federation, Inc.
P.O. Box 2714
Dunedin, FL 34697

Shotokan Karate of America
222 S. Hewitt Street, Room 7
Los Angeles, CA 90012
Telephone: (213) 437-0988

USA Karate Federation, Inc.
1300 Kenmore Blvd.
Akron, OH 44314
Telephone: (330) 753-3114

INDEX